D1550996

EXCEPTIONAL LATINOS

SONIA SOTOMAYOR

Supreme Court Justice

Stephanie
Sammartino McPherson

Enslow Publishing
101 W. 23rd Street
Suite 240
New York, NY 10011
USA

enslow.com

Words to Know

court—A place where questions about law are decided.

federal—Having to do with the country's government rather than state government.

Hispanic—A person of Spanish-speaking background.

justice—A judge on the Supreme Court.

lawyer—A person who argues cases in court.

minority—A Hispanic, African American, or other non-white person.

nominate—To suggest someone for a job.

press conference—A public announcement to news reporters.

prosecutor—A lawyer who works to send people accused of crimes to jail.

strike—Workers' refusal to continue a job until they get more money or better hours.

Supreme Court—The highest federal court in the United States made up of nine justices.

Contents

Sonia Sotomayor

CHAPTER 1

"The Greatest Gift"

Sonia Sotomayor was born on June 25, 1954. Her parents, Celina and Juan, came from Puerto Rico but met in the United States. They lived in a rough part of New York City called the Bronx.

Sonia was a bold little girl. If anyone tried to bully her little brother, Juan Junior, she fought for him. Sonia's hero, teenage detective Nancy Drew, also stood up for people. Reading Nancy Drew books made Sonia want to join the police force someday.

Young Sonia poses with her parents. They were both from Puerto Rico and the family often went back there for visits.

Sonia Says:

"Our books, especially the encyclopedia, were like a window into another world."

Sonia's mother made sure there were plenty of other books in the house too, including an encyclopedia. "My mother gave us the greatest gift," Sonia would later say. "An education."

Sonia's Life Changes

Sonia attended a very good Catholic school. One day during Mass at school, Sonia fainted. The teachers rushed her to the hospital. After some medical tests, a doctor said that Sonia had diabetes.

A person with diabetes has dangerous changes in his or her blood sugar. Every day Sonia needed a shot to keep her blood sugar at the right level. At seven years old, Sonia learned to give the shot to herself.

Diabetes changed Sonia's life in another way too. Doctors told her she could never become a police officer. But watching the television show *Perry Mason* about a **lawyer** who solved crimes gave Sonia another idea. If she couldn't be a "cop," she would become a lawyer.

As a little girl, Sonia spoke Spanish with her family. She did not start speaking English well until she was about nine years old.

CHAPTER 2

Busy Years

When she was a senior in high school, Sonia applied to Princeton University. Even though she was an excellent student, others had come from better schools. Sonia got into the school with the help of a program called affirmative action. This gave special treatment to **minority** students such as African Americans and **Hispanics**. Many of these children had grown up poor and did not have the same chances as white children.

Sonia graduated from the eighth grade at the top of her class.

The Top of the Class

At first, Sonia felt out of place at Princeton. But Sonia did not get discouraged. She studied hard, spent lots of time in the library, and asked teachers for extra help. Sonia made top grades and joined groups that helped Latino students.

Sonia attended Princeton University from 1972 until 1976.

When she graduated in 1976, the university awarded her highest honors.

The next few years were busy. Sonia married her high school boyfriend, Kevin Noonan. She graduated from Yale Law School, and she started her first job in New York. As a public **prosecutor**, she helped send criminals to jail.

Sonia Says:

"For me, it [affirmative action] was a door opener that changed the course of my life."

CHAPTER 3

A Hard Worker

By 1984 Sonia's life had changed again. She and Kevin had divorced, and she was working at a private law firm. Sonia helped protect people's ideas from being stolen or copied. She also did a great deal of public service work. People began to take note of her success—even in the White House.

In 1991 President George H. W. Bush **nominated** Sonia to be a **federal** district judge. When someone asked her if learning to be a judge would be hard, Sonia replied, "I've spent

President Bush nominated Sonia to be a federal district judge in 1991. She was the youngest judge on the court.

my whole life learning how to do things that were hard for me. None of it has been easy." But hard work never bothered Sonia.

Sonia Becomes a Judge

Sonia became New York's first Hispanic federal judge on August 12, 1992. One of her most famous cases had to do with a baseball **strike**

Yankee Stadium stands empty in 1994 because of a baseball strike. Sonia helped put an end to the strike in 1995.

in 1995. There had been no games for eight months. Sonia ended the strike, and games started up. Fans all over the country could enjoy baseball again.

Sonia moved on to a higher **court** in 1998. Federal courts have three levels. A person who loses in a lower court may take his case to the next higher level. For ten years, Sonia reviewed over three thousand decisions made by lower courts. Her energy seemed boundless.

Sonia Says:

"I have a streak of stubbornness in me that I think has accounted for some of my success in life."

CHAPTER 4

"The People's Justice"

On May 26, 2009, Sonia stood beside President Barack Obama at a White House **press conference**. The president announced that he was nominating Sonia for the **Supreme Court**. "She's faced down barriers," the president said, "overcome the odds, lived out the American dream."

Sonia's dream had taken her to the highest court in the land. Soon she was discussing many issues with her fellow **justices**. These included

President Obama nominated Sonia to be the first Hispanic justice on the US Supreme Court.

Sonia Says:

> "I . . . . believe those of us who have opportunities in this life must give back to those who have less."

affirmative action, health care, voting rights, and many others. Sonia asked tough questions to get to the heart of each case. She stood up for her beliefs when she disagreed with the other judges.

Working for Others

Despite everything that she has done, Sonia is a down-to-earth person who understands the problems of ordinary citizens. News reporters call her "the people's justice."

Sonia's popularity has led her to some interesting places. She threw the first pitch for the New York Yankees in 2009. She made several appearances on *Sesame Street*. She even swore in Joe Biden as vice president on January 21, 2013.

What matters most to Sonia, however, has always been making things better for others.

Before throwing out the first pitch, Sonia is led on to the field by Yankees catcher Jorge Posada.

Sonia, top right, stands with the other members of the Supreme Court.

"I understood the lawyer's job as being to help people," she wrote in her book. "I understood the law as a force for good." Whatever the future holds, Sonia will continue to fight for justice for everyone.

Timeline

1954—Sonia is born on June 25.

1976—Sonia graduates from Princeton University with honors.

1979—Sonia graduates from Yale Law School.

1979—Sonia becomes a public prosecutor in New York.

1984—Sonia joins a private law firm.

1992—Sonia becomes a federal district judge.

1995—Sonia ends an eight-month baseball strike.

1998—Sonia becomes a judge in the US Court of Appeals.

2009—President Obama nominates Sonia for the Supreme Court on May 26. The Senate confirms Sonia's nomination on August 6.

2013—Sonia swears in Vice President Joe Biden on January 21.

Learn More

Books

Anderson, Annmarie. *When I Grow Up: Sonia Sotomayor*. New York: Scholastic, 2014.

Krull, Kathleen. *Women Who Broke the Rules: Sonia Sotomayor*. New York: Bloomsbury USA, 2015.

Rose, Simon. *Supreme Court*. New York: Weigl, 2014.

Winter, Jonah, and Edel Rodriquez. *A Judge Grows in the Bronx/La Juez Que Crecio En El Bronx*. New York: Atheneum Books, 2009.

Web Sites

congressforkids.net/Judicialbranch_supremecourt.htm
Explains the Supreme Court and provides interesting facts, a fun quiz, and project ideas.

bensguide.gpo.gov/9-12/government/national/scourt.html
Covers how the Supreme Court works and provides a link to the official Supreme Court Web site.

kidsdiscover.com/spotlight/supreme-court-kids/
Discusses history and major cases of the Supreme Court and includes interesting photos.

Index

To Dick

Published in 2016 by Enslow Publishing, LLC.
101 W. 23rd Street, Suite 240, New York, NY 10011

Copyright © 2016 by Enslow Publishing, LLC.

All rights reserved.

No part of this book may be reproduced by any means
without the written permission of the publisher.

Cataloging-in-Publication Data
McPherson, Stephanie Sammartino.
Sonia Sotomayor: Supreme Court justice / by Stephanie
Sammartino McPherson.
p. cm.—(Exceptional Latinos)
Includes bibliographical references and index.
ISBN 978-0-7660-6724-0 (library binding)
ISBN 978-0-7660-6722-6 (pbk.)
ISBN 978-0-7660-6723-3 (6-pack)
1. Sotomayor, Sonia,—1954—Juvenile literature. 2.
Hispanic American judges —Biography—Juvenile
literature. 3. Judges—United States—Biography—
Juvenile literature. I. McPherson, Stephanie Sammartino.
II. Title.
KF8745.S67 M395 2016
347.73'2634—d23

Printed in the United States of America

To Our Readers: We have done our best to make sure
all Web site addresses in this book were active and
appropriate when we went to press. However, the author
and the publisher have no control over and assume no
liability for the material available on those Web sites
or on any Web sites they may link to. Any comments or
suggestions can be sent by e-mail to customerservice@
enslow.com.

Photo Credits: © AP Images, pp. 15, 20; Chip Somodevilla/
Getty Images. p. 18; Diana Walker/ The LIFE images
Collection/Getty Images, p. 14; MANDEL NGAN/AFP/
Getty Images, p. 4; Mark Wilson/Getty Images News/
Getty Images, p. 21; MCT/Tribune News Service/Getty
Images (Sonia Sotomayor), p. 1; Oliver Morris/Hulton
Archive/Getty Images, p. 11; Toria/Shutterstock.com (blue
background); © White House Press Office/ZUMA press, pp.
6, 8, 10.

Cover Credits: MCT/Tribune News Service/Getty Images
(Sonia Sotomayor); Toria/Shutterstock.com (blue
background).